Save Our COASTS!

Sarah Fleming

Junior School Resource

OXFORD
UNIVERSITY PRESS

OXFORD
UNIVERSITY PRESS

Great Clarendon Street, Oxford OX2 6DP

Oxford University Press is a department of the University of Oxford.
It furthers the University's objective of excellence in research, scholarship,
and education by publishing worldwide in

Oxford   New York

Auckland   Cape Town   Dar es Salaam   Hong Kong   Karachi
Kuala Lumpur   Madrid   Melbourne   Mexico City   Nairobi
New Delhi   Shanghai   Taipei   Toronto

With offices in

Argentina   Austria   Brazil   Chile   Czech Republic   France   Greece
Guatemala   Hungary   Italy   Japan   Poland   Portugal   Singapore
South Korea   Switzerland   Thailand   Turkey   Ukraine   Vietnam

Oxford is a registered trade mark of Oxford University Press
in the UK and in certain other countries

Text © Sarah Fleming 2005

The moral rights of the author have been asserted

Database right Oxford University Press (maker)

First published 2005

British Library Cataloguing in Publication Data

Data available

ISBN 978-0-19-919876-4

21 23 25 27 29 30 28 26 24 22

Printed in China by Imago

Paper used in the production of this book is a natural,
recyclable product made from wood grown in sustainable forests.
The manufacturing process conforms to the environmental
regulations of the country of origin.

Acknowledgements

The publisher would like to thank the following for permission to reproduce
photographs: **p3** Corbis/Ric Ergenbright; **p4**t Corbis, b Alamy/Andrew Seale; **p5** Corbis/Philip
James Corwin; **p6**t Corbis/Clay Perry, c Corbis/Michael S Yamoshita, b Corbis/Niall Benvie; **p7**
Corbis/Julia Waterlow/Eye Ubiquitous; **p8** Corbis/Steve Kaufman; **p10** Event
Photography/Photographers Direct; **p11** Corbis/Dean Conger; **p13**t Corbis/Yann Arthus-Bertand,
b Corbis/Georgia Lowell; **p14**t Corbis/Yann Arthus-Bertand, b Biorock Communications/Wolf
Hilbertz; **p15** Biorock Communications/Wolf Hilbertz; **p17** Corbis/Tanya Arruza; **p18** Corbis;
p19t Science Photo Library/NASA, b Corbis/Lloyd Duff; **p20**t Corbis/Reza Webistan, b Christine
Osborne Pictures/Photographers Direct; **p21** Corbis/Reza Webistan; **p25** Corbis/Michael
Nicholson; **p26**t Corbis/Natalie Forbes, b Corbis/Niall Benvie; **p27**t Corbis/Bryn
Colton/Assignments Photographers, b Corbis/Roger Tidman; **p28**t Corbis/Jonathan Blair, b
Corbis/Pizzoli Alberto/Sygma; **p29** digitalglobe.com; **p30**t Corbis/Henry Romero/Reuters, b
Corbis/Picimpact; **p31**t Corbis/Sygma, b Topham Picturepoint

Cover photography: Corbis/David Sailors

Illustrations by Martin Cottam: **p23**; Mark Duffin: **p3**, **p4**, **p8**, **p9**, **p10**, **p11**, **p12**, **p16**, **p17**,
p18, **p22**, **p24**, **p29**

Contents

Changing coasts   4

What have we done?   6

Rising sea levels   8

Changing sea levels over time   10

Reef coast: the Maldives   12

Beach coast: the east coast of the USA   16

River delta: the Nile   19

Low-lying coast: The Netherlands   22

Case Study: storms and flooding   24

Sinking city: Venice   28

Earthquake   29

Extreme weather   30

Glossary/Index   32

15m
X7

The White Cliffs of Dover are about 100 metres high. That's roughly the same height as seven 4-storey buildings. Look out for the building icon throughout the book to help you compare heights.

Changing coasts

Coasts are where seas and oceans meet land. There are many types of coast.

Sand, gravel or muddy beaches cover 75% of the world's coasts – the rest are cliffs.

The Bay of Fundy in Canada has the biggest tide in the world. Sea level at low tide is 45m lower than at high tide.

The roots of the mangrove tree provide a **habitat** for animals, and keep the sandy soil from being swept away by tides.

Cliff coasts tend to be younger shorelines, made of rocks which haven't yet had time to be battered by the sea.

Coasts are being battered all the time by winds and waves causing **erosion**. This is a natural process – coasts have always changed over time. But some coasts change more quickly because of what people do.

The shape of coastlines depends on:

- waves
- type of rock
- tides
- river mouths
- ice
- wind
- people
- and global warming.

The last two can lead to coasts changing rapidly. Many people live on or near coastlines, so coastal changes can affect people's lives. This book looks at some coastal situations and how people are managing coastal change.

What have we done?

Humans interfere with natural water cycles that affect coasts in many ways.

Directly affecting coasts

We:

- build artificial ports, changing the sea's natural currents and tides

- change coastlines, and even create new ones

- trample over sand dunes, wearing them down, then winds and waves hit the coast with much more force

Mountains on two islands were flattened and put into the sea to make an artificial island for Hong Kong's new airport. 5km of new coast was made.

- try to stop the sea from eroding coasts.

Indirectly affecting coasts

We change rivers, and this affects the water flowing out of the river mouths at coasts. We:

- dam rivers, which changes the flow and stops **silt** in river water going downstream

- take water out of rivers to use for ourselves, so less water flows into the seas. Habitats such as salt marshes at river mouths dry up, killing the wildlife that lives there

- use fertilizers, which seep through soil into rivers. There the chemicals kill fish and encourage water plants to grow. These can choke rivers

- pollute rivers with chemicals from cities and industry.

Finally, we burn **fossil fuels** such as oil, coal and gas. Scientists think this is making the world's atmosphere warm up.

So much water is taken out of the Yellow River in China for people, industry and farming that the lower end of the river runs dry for three to four months of the year.

Rising sea levels

Sea levels on Earth are linked with temperature. The Earth's temperature changes all the time. It changes in a yearly cycle from winter to summer, but it also has a cycle of colder and hotter periods that last hundreds of thousands of years. For example, there has been an Ice Age about once every 100,000 years.

When the Earth gets cold, the sea level drops. This is because water on land freezes and stops flowing into the sea.

When the Earth gets hotter, the sea level rises because the sea's volume increases. This can happen in two ways:

- the sea gets warmer so the water expands. The same amount of water takes up more space as it heats up

- ice on land melts and extra water flows into the sea. Water melts that was frozen and 'trapped' as ice on land in glaciers (flowing ice rivers) and in ice sheets (huge areas of ice).

If all the glaciers melted, the sea level would rise by about 0.3 metres.

This glacier flows down to the coast of Argentina from the Patagonian ice sheet in South America.

The biggest ice sheets are on the Antarctic (which is a land continent) and Greenland. If they melted completely, the sea level on Earth would rise by 80 metres.

new sea level

80 m

current sea level

The Myth

Sea levels *won't* rise if ice at the North Pole melts. This is because the ice is floating on the sea. When ice melts into water, the volume gets smaller, and it just fills the space it was floating in.

← This much ice →

Sea level stays the same

...melts to make this much water →

Changing sea levels over time

Sea levels on Earth have changed many times in the past, as the Earth's temperature has gone up and down very slowly. During the last Ice Age 20,000 years ago, sea levels were 125 metres lower than they are now.

The Earth has also been hotter than it is today, and sea levels have been as much as 20 metres higher than they are now.

The sea was up here – this used to be a beach!

The problem for people

Humans have evolved in quite a cool period of the Earth's history. The Earth is still hotting up from the last Ice Age. Many scientists think that people are making the Earth heat up faster by burning fossil fuels.

In the last 100 years, the average temperature of the Earth has gone up by about 1°Celsius and sea levels have risen about 2–3 millimetres a year. Scientists say that this rate of change is going to speed up.

The problem for people is that changing sea levels threaten the lives of those who live near coasts.

What will happen to these homes if sea levels rise?

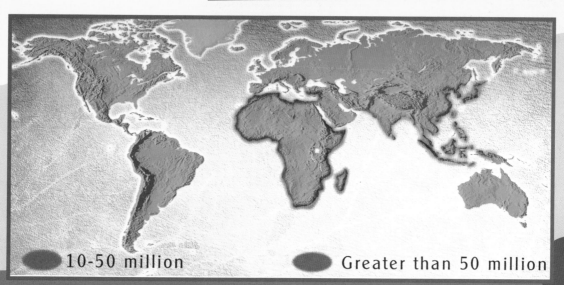

10-50 million   Greater than 50 million

Numbers of people living near coasts who may be affected by rising sea levels.

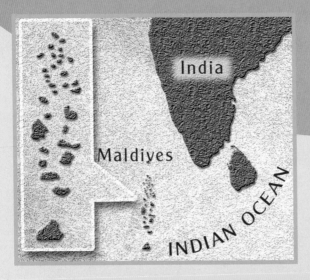

Place	Indian Ocean
Number of islands	1192
Inhabited islands	202
Highest point	2.4m

The area

The Maldive Islands are mainly made of coast. People go there for tropical holidays – sun, sea and sand.

The science: waves

Big waves build up a lot of energy as they cross the ocean.

The Maldives are protected from big waves by their coral reefs. The underwater reefs block the waves' paths, taking energy out of them. They turn **destructive**, high-energy waves into gentle, low-energy ones before they reach the coasts.

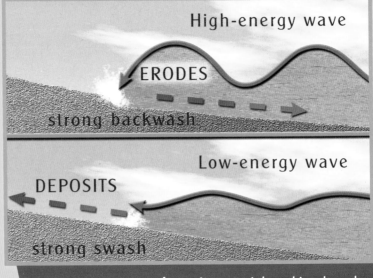

High-energy waves erode beaches or cliffs, taking material away with their strong **backwash**.

Low-energy waves **deposit** material, making beaches as they drop material in their strong **swash**.

island

deep water

shallow water

coral reef

The energy of the waves hitting these islands is **absorbed** by the coral reefs.

The problem

Parts of the coral reefs that surrounded some of the inhabited islands have been dug up. The coral is used to make walls and buildings. This has destroyed the habitat of the animals that make the sand, and has let high-energy waves reach the coasts. Beaches are disappearing and homes are at risk from large waves.

Tree roots are exposed as the beaches are eroded.

The Maldives' capital city, Male (say 'Ma-lay'), covers the whole of an island called Male. Male's reefs were dug up to make buildings, so it had no defence against the sea. In 1987 and 1991 the island was flooded by large waves. Something had to be done.

The solutions

1 A concrete wall has been built in the sea all round Male, to replace the coral reef. You can see the waves breaking against the wall, not on the island. Even this wall was unable to stop the huge waves that flooded Male in December 2004, but it did absorb most of their power, and so saved many lives.

2 Some Maldive islands are protected by cages of dead coral. The cages slow down the waves. But these cages rust and fall apart. They have to be replaced every five years.

3 Around one Maldive island metal grids have been placed in the water, and a tiny electric current is run through them. Deposits grow on the framework and corals grow on them. The electric current also helps coral grow quickly. Over time, animals come back, and beaches are remade.

This is a better solution than the walls or cages. Reefs re-grow and animals return. Beaches and islands are protected. And it's prettier! But it is expensive, so it is not yet being widely used.

This coral grows quickly and can cope better with global warming.

Rising sea levels – more problems

If sea levels rise too quickly, reefs won't be able to grow fast enough to stay near the surface and may die. If sea levels rise too high, low-lying islands, like the Maldives, may disappear completely.

The area

All down the Atlantic coast of the United States of America there are very large cities and big ports which affect the way the ocean meets the coast. Lots of people live in homes on beach fronts along this coast.

On the east coast of the USA, the wind blows from the north, so sand is pushed down the coast from the north to the south by longshore drift. This is a natural cycle. Sand that is washed south from beaches is replaced by new sand from the north.

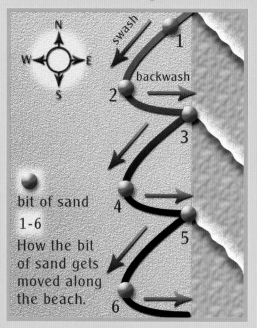

The science: longshore drift

bit of sand

1-6

How the bit of sand gets moved along the beach.

When the main winds and currents hit a coast at an angle, material making up the shore – sand or pebbles – is pushed down the coast.

The problem

Sea walls, groynes, buildings, ports – blockages of all kinds – get in the way of longshore drift. Sand builds up to the north of the blockages, and is not moved on further south. Beaches are being eroded away by up to 1 metre a year. 170,000 homes on the coast are in danger.

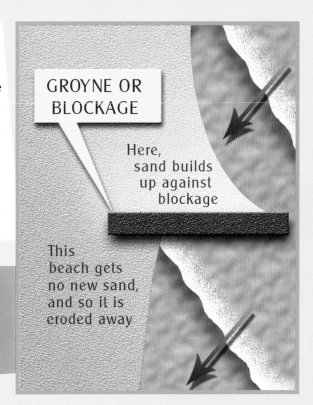

GROYNE OR BLOCKAGE

Here, sand builds up against blockage

This beach gets no new sand, and so it is eroded away

A groyne is a wooden wall put on a beach to stop longshore drift. Sand piles against one side of it. Sand further down the beach is still eroded.

The east coast of the USA is also hit by hurricanes. With no beach to slow the hurricanes down when they arrive from the sea, they do even more damage to property.

The solutions

1 Make sand dunes in front of buildings. Sea grasses help to stop sand from being eroded away. The roots hold the sand in place and the leaves slow down the winds.

2 Make artificial reefs out at sea to slow down waves and get them to deposit more sand.

3 Add extra sand to the disappearing beaches.

Tube covered with sand and planted with sea grass

Tube of special plastic

Tube filled with sand and water mix

River delta: the Nile

The Nile used to flood once a year, depositing **fertile silt** on the Egyptian valley. Farming this rich soil helped the Ancient Egyptians become wealthy and build a powerful civilization.

The Nile slows down in its final stages. It flows into a fan of channels – a 160km long **delta** – into the Mediterranean sea.

The Nile is one of the longest rivers in the world.

Mediterranean Sea

Delta

Cairo

River Nile

Red Sea

EGYPT

Aswan Dam

The Aswan Dam was built in 1971.

A huge dam was built on the Nile to provide **hydroelectric power** and keep the level of the Nile more even throughout the year, which helps shipping and industry. The government can let more water out of the dam to flood farmland if flooding is needed. But the silt in the Nile's water hits the dam and sinks. It cannot get past the dam. So the Nile valley below the Aswan Dam is no longer rich farming land.

The problems

- Some of the silt used to be deposited at the delta, making up for erosion of the delta by the sea. But now the dam blocks the silt and with no new deposits, the sea is eroding the delta at the rate of between 30–200 metres a year.

- 70% of Egypt's 77 million people live in the delta.

Since the Aswan Dam has been built, the sea is advancing and has destroyed many houses.

- To feed all the people there is a lot of farming. But because the dam has stopped the rich silt deposits, people use lots of chemical fertilizers. These seep into water channels and:
  - encourage water plants to grow so much that they block the channels
  - pollute the water and kill fish
  - damage people's health.

Water plants are a huge problem in the delta's waterway.

Fresh water is taken from the Nile for people, farming and industry.

- Today only 10% of the water in the Nile reaches the sea. Because so little fresh water flows into the sea it is getting saltier. This is damaging habitats all round the eastern Mediterranean. Salt water is also seeping into the delta, making farming even more difficult.

The solution

Egypt has put in some coastal defences, but solutions still need to be found to save the Nile delta from erosion and pollution.

Low-lying coast: The Netherlands

The Netherlands

Today, over 40% of The Netherlands is land that has been taken from the North Sea. Much of this reclaimed land lies below sea level, the lowest being 7 metres below the sea!

The pale blue areas on this map used to be low-lying coasts made up of salt marshes and bogs. Until people interfered, only little islands of higher ground rose above the marshes.

The Dutch have made their country bigger by taking land from the sea for over two thousand years.

NORTH SEA

The Netherlands

Germ

Amsterdam

Belgium

Land below sea level

To do so they build **dykes** (walls) in the sea and then pump water away from the land behind the wall. The dykes used to be earth walls full of rocks, with gravel sides facing the sea. Now they are concrete and rock. The pumps used to be powered by windmills, now they are pumped by electricity.

Sea

Dyke

Reclaimed fields below sea level

Sometimes dykes collapsed, flooding fields and villages. 10,000 people died in one storm in 1421 as the North Sea broke through dykes in The Netherlands.

Case study: storms and flooding

On 31st January 1953 a great storm swept north up the west coast of Scotland, and round into the North Sea. A **surge** of huge waves swept down the North Sea, flooding parts of the eastern United Kingdom and The Netherlands.

The storm of 1953.

BIG WAVE SURGE

NORTH SEA

Northern Ireland

United Kingdom

The Netherlands

Between Stranraer and Northern Ireland: 133 die as ferry sinks.

North Norfolk: 80 die as sea embankments collapse.

Clacton: 35 people drown as sea rises 1m in 15 minutes.

Canvey Island: Sea walls collapse. 58 die.

50 dykes burst and the sea claimed back 9% of The Netherlands.

The storm of 1953

The storm of 1953 was one of the worst storms in the area in the 20th century.

The Netherlands: 1,835 people drowned and 46,000 houses were damaged.

UK: In all, 300 people drowned and 24,000 houses were damaged.

The solutions

The death and destruction caused by that storm led governments in both countries to:

- build flood barriers to protect large cities.
- improve early warning systems for storms and floods.

Early warning systems allow time to put defences in place. The 1953 flood made the UK government look at ways of protecting low-lying London from future flooding. One of the measures, the Thames Barrier, was completed in 1984. This has 'doors' which can be closed to stop flood waters reaching London.

New solutions

Building a sea wall costs over three million pounds a kilometre. Although a sea wall protects the area behind it, it can make erosion worse further along the coast.

New tactics are constantly being tried out in the battle with the sea. As well as active defences such as sea walls and groynes, a new tactic called **managed retreat** is being tried out.

DANGER
THESE DUNES ARE BEING UNDERMINED BY COASTAL EROSION, ANY ACTIVITIES NEAR STEEP FACE OF SAND DUNES COULD BE DANGEROUS

Some houses are being left to fall into the sea.

The idea is that in the end we can't stop the sea, so it would be better to let the sea have the land back in a way that causes the least damage to people and property.

In some areas of the UK the sea is being allowed to re-enter areas that used to be protected with sea walls. Land which had been reclaimed for farming is returning to natural salt marshes. The salt marshes will be a natural barrier between people and the sea. They help to slow down storms and provide a place for water to collect.

Salt marshes also create a haven for wildlife.

Sinking city: Venice

The city of Venice, in Italy, is sinking and sea levels are rising – a double problem.

Sinking

Venice is built on millions of wooden stilts that were hammered into marshy ground over a thousand years ago. The weight of the buildings sitting on the stilts make them sink further into the marsh at a rate of about 7 centimetres per 100 years – that's 70 centimetres since they were first built.

Sea rising

It is estimated that the sea around Venice will rise by 50–100 centimetres in the next 100 years.

The city of Venice is putting huge barriers in the sea around Venice to protect it.

Venice, with its 200 canals and over 400 bridges, was built on a marsh.

For the last 30 years, Venice has been flooded by over 1 m of sea water in winter months. Will it survive another 30 years?

Earthquake

Large earthquakes under the sea can make huge, powerful waves called tsunamis. Tsunamis travel over the ocean at speeds of up to 500 kilometres per hour and can sweep over coasts up to 1.6 kilometres inland, destroying everything in their paths.

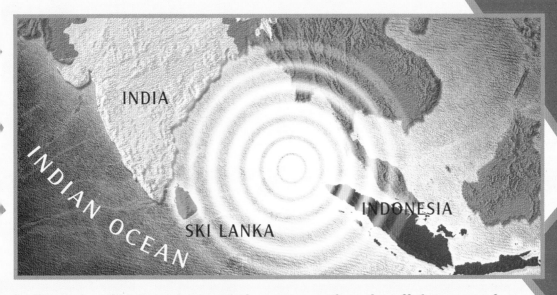

In December 2004 a massive underwater earthquake off the coast of Indonesia created huge tsunamis. These crashed into the coasts of ten countries around the Indian Ocean, killing nearly 300,000 people.

Can you see what the tsunami pulled back out to sea with it after it struck?

Aceh, in Indonesia, before the tsunami.

Aceh after the tsunami.

Extreme weather

As well as sea levels rising, another effect of global warming is that weather is likely to become more extreme. What used to be unusual bad weather – storms, droughts, flooding – will become more common.

Many of the effects of extreme bad weather are felt mostly on coasts.

- Storms usually start at sea. Storm-force winds gather energy as they speed across water. When a storm reaches land, the energy is used in destroying the coast and anything it finds there. As storms move inland they calm down.

- Giant waves can destroy coastal defences, erode beaches, eat cliffs and batter headlands.

- Tidal surges flood coastal areas. Low-lying coastal land can get covered in salt, which ruins any farming in the area and makes fresh water salty.

Sea defences may not be able to cope.

In 2004 six major hurricanes swept through the Caribbean sea and on to the USA. Normally there are only two or three a year.

Scientists say that:

- big waves beating coasts will become more common
- the weather in the UK will become wetter and colder in the winter, and hotter and drier in the summer
- tornadoes, hurricanes and other violent storms will become more common all over the world
- flooding caused by tidal surges will happen more often and be more severe.

Bangladesh, 1991. Over 125,000 people were killed by a huge tidal wave.

Governments all over the world are trying to slow down global warming by changing laws about burning fossil fuels. Are they too late?

Glossary

absorb – to soak up

backwash – the movement of a wave going away from a coast

delta – a triangular area at the mouth of a river where it spreads into branches

deposit – put something down

destructive – destroying

dyke – a barrier or long embankment against flooding

erode – wear away

fertile silt – rich material laid down by a river that produces good crops

fossil fuels – a natural fuel such as coal or gas formed in the geological past

habitat – where a plant or animal lives naturally

hydroelectric power – electricity produced using water

managed retreat – to go backwards from an existing defence line in an organized way

silt – material from a river

surge – a sudden and powerful move forwards or upwards

swash – the movement of a wave going up on to a coast

Index

beaches   4, 10, 12, 13, 15, 16–18, 30

cliffs   4, 5, 24, 30

coral reef   12–15

delta   19–21

dykes   22–23

East Coast, USA   16–18

erosion   5, 6, 12, 17, 18, 20, 21, 30

global warming   5, 7, 10, 11, 31

groyne   17, 26

hurricane   17, 31

ice   5, 8, 10, 11

longshore drift   16–17

Maldives, The   12–15

Netherlands, The   22–25

Nile, The   19–21

rising sea levels   5, 8, 9, 10, 11, 15, 28, 30

storms   14, 23, 24, 25, 26, 29, 30, 31

tsunami   29

United Kingdom   24–25, 27

Venice   28

wall (sea)   14, 15, 22, 26